T0137524

Cat Bones

joan cofrancesco

authorHOUSE®

AuthorHouse™
1663 Liberty Drive
Bloomington, IN 47403
www.authorhouse.com
Phone: 1 (800) 839-8640

Cover Art by Devon Seifer.

Published by AuthorHouse 11/14/2017

ISBN: 978-1-5462-1724-4 (sc)
ISBN: 978-1-5462-1743-5 (e)

Print information available on the last page.

This book is printed on acid-free paper.

"Cats are spontaneous, content to live in the present moment. They're small, shedding, scratching, inscrutable Zen masters sent to teach us the paradox of undoing in a hectic world where things always have to be done. As balls of fur presently curled up on my desk clearly demonstrates, the more naps you take, the more awakenings you experience. Animals are our spiritual companions."

--*Simple Abundance: A Daybook of Comfort & Joy*
Sara Ban Breathnach

"Whether they are Bukowski's or your own, cats have become a mysterious presence in your poems. They are your talismans."

--Howard Nelson

This book is dedicated
to my Muse
and Companion in Hell

Year of the Cat

C A T

B O N E S

IN   THE   TREE

THE   FIRE   DEPARTMENT

N

E

V

E

R

C A M E

The Virtues of Having
Cats as Pets

1. They don't argue.

2. They don't ask for money.

3. They don't stay out
   until 2AM   then lie to
   you about where they've been.

4. They sleep with you
   no matter what.

5. They listen to Vivaldi.

6. They don't talk in their sleep.

7. They let you write poems about them
   without explanation.

My Name is Alice
And I Am Hemingway's Cat

The tea boils
My eyes squint on the red sofa
overlooking the sea

mistresses come
and go

you are waking
from another drunken dream
your wife is pale
as she sips her orange tea

my nose on her leg does not console
mistresses come
and go

I roll in the sun on the sheets then
paw at the bedroom mirror
as I still smell the mistresses sprawled out, naked legs
on the bed, a scratchy Bolero
on the stereo and Jack Daniels spilled
on her dress.

I know when rats die
I see their ghosts in particles of air
your son hates you
Gertrude is mad again
what did you call her last night…?

a new day heats my fur
as I arch and stretch
I want to scratch walls
piss on your first edition of THE OLD MAN
I pray you never
squeeze your big trigger at me
But it's big pussys that you like anyway

mistresses come
and go

i hear the huge bed squeaking
in the room above
I see you Ernest
as a blind sportsman who has lost
his canoe
gun
love
sun
control
soul

Please circle one.

4AM

Without a doubt,
this is my undoing.
Watching the last
flickers of Christmas   Night
Maddipal incense,
the confusing
jangle of a Mile's   tune
thirsting for a sip
of wine,
holding an empty
glass.

Pulling the House Around Me
Like an Old Afghan

Because the winter days are short
I will sleep throughout this morning
light a single candle
pull the first cold sheets of December
over my head.

This is where I jump-start my life stealing
dreams from Bukowski's cats
who come in to sit by the flame—
three pairs of green eyes staring.

He Must Have Been a Buddha
In One of His 9-Lives

My cat has
a grand quality
about him
when he sits motionless across
from me at my desk
like a Buddha
for hours
moving only to stretch and spread
his paws slowly across
the white paper
with a precision
and grace
usually reserved
for more
majestic
things.

The Geometry of My Pear-
Shaped Cat

My pear shaped cat
batting
nip

between his 7-toed black
paws
under

falling octagon framed painting
of cat frantically chasing
25 cool ocean-
colored
pears

is enough
$$cat^2 = \sqrt{\text{pear-shaped}^{25} \text{ x7 toes}}$$
for one

Sunday
afternoon.

Poem to Raymond Carver

comforter thrown
over my legs
late morning
cats asleep at my feet
I am reading a tattered copy
of A NEW PATH TO THE WATERFALL
you said you wanted this
all of your life
waking each day to
everything new
choosing whether to
fish or write of play
with your cat Morris
I look outside at the new snow—
the same Syracuse snow
that you must have watched
and I too feel like
lobotomizing the morning
rising only to cook brook trout
for breakfast.

Mysteries

Marijuana
Marley on the stereo
S+M dreams   all night
snow riding over and
down to the lake

living room has
Ted and Mary reading
Tarot cards
surrounding themselves
with candles
and secret rituals

I hang garlic around
my neck to ward off
evil.

the black cats lick
each other's balls

if you can't be free
sd Dove,   be a
mystery.

Are You Warm Enough,
Or Shall I Put Another Log in the Fire?
Part II
  (to Andy)

I search
        and
I search some more.

            I'm lucky
            or
            I'm not,
            it varies.

        I prefer a life filled
        with

            the possibility of winning the lottery
            the randomness of clothes on a line
            the mystery of the existence of some other world
            the choice of Frost's paths in the woods
            the alternative ways to find Outer Mongolia
                    on a world atlas
            the variety of reincarnations in my life.

But I'll still go home
Because sometimes
I need to find the butter
in
the compartment marked
                    butter.

Another 4AM Poem

I set the alarm at 4AM
to drive to
Provincetown

cats walk the slats
of the city morning
in summer
fight on the fire-escape
I disregard them
but pack my Nike sneakers,
beach ball, Cosmic Mama's Magic
Brownies, maps

The light comes
into my window
wavering over my world
of blues,
Jazz, and old photos

I can hear someone
else's TV
as I pack my car

soon I will be there—
washing the city sounds
into the ocean.

20 Degrees Below Zero

warm me with some old Byrd jazz
under the Catskill spell
as I sit by my Bullard woodstove
in my flannel shirt from LL
Bean. As cows lie down in snow
turtles in ancient shells.

Company on Christmas Eve

I chop the vegetables
carrots   onions   celery   garlic   bell
peppers
Orvieto on ice, fish on platters
red wine breathing
on the counter
10,000 maniacs unplugged
on the stereo
china from grumps
cats stretched out
under the 5-foot balsam.

rituals bind
humanity
yet I enjoy
these simple things
Red candles.   Warm Italian
bread.   A knock
at the door.

Pap Smear
(revised)

I mount the table
push my feet into stirrups—
you in your starched white
adjust your miner's light
stare into labyrinths
smooth on sterile
flexam
latex gloves
slide in thick tongs   spread them
take it easy
I look upside down
at your framed diploma
You look at my vagina
no licks or caresses
                    only
steel.

Leaping

the way the black cat stretches
on the Oriental rug
with a small red rice paper journal
from Nepal
in his teeth

the way Robert Bly's poetry leaps
from snowy fields to
ants to Vietnam

the way she moves
like a panther
head tilted over
the worn leather of a red
1964 MG convertible

is way enough
Zen for me.

Voo-doo

In the bedroom filled with cats
and ocean breezes, the talk of Colette,
sexual acts of imagination
that fan us with smells
as potent as jasmine

I am rolling my own.
The pot and sweat smell
in the clothes we rip off.
Inside the Coke bottle
by the bed
a violet.
Our skin laps smooth between blue
satin sheets.

Cats flow by my talismans
working their magic to keep you here
their victim locked in drums, chants, smells
of blood and incense, and wine.

Simplifying My Life

Reading the ancient runes.   Be
tween barns my Saab sits
rusting under moonlight.

Licking the Pages

> "Our perfect companions never
> have fewer than four feet."—Colette

Like Colette's cats
sensuous purring
rubbing up against her satin
pillowcases
sprawling out on queen-
sized beds

I too love her
keep her photo standing
upright on my tigeroak bureau
keep a candle burning before it
in a most holy manner
of sweet regard

In the fragrance of rose
I slow dance naked
in my Victorian bedroom
to the music,
"moonlight serenade"
on a 1920 Victrola

In this world of loving men and women
I have lived between one world
and then another. Arms into arms,
tongues into tongues.

I want to live every day
   in ecstasy
        firing through
          my nine lives
            until there is nothing left.

Winter Massage

Zane Grey hardcovers on the shelf
apple wood in stove crackling

sun on snow covered mountains
icicles shining on firs

bottle of Beaujolais cold
wind blowing under the door

Manx cat lying on Persian rug
beside the CATSKILL NEWS

softly distant drums from new
world music CD chanting

winter's ordinary smells
balsam and cedar incense

Unassuming and perfect
soft body on futon

waiting for hands

Walking A Thin Line
  (to rossiter)

I watch old reruns
of Saturday Night Live
read last weeks Sunday journal
put extra grass in the BONG
and hope
it's not too much

too much poetry,
pot, 10,000 MANIACS
and I'll end up
sleeping with Rip
in the forest

My lover and cats
in another dimension
dreaming of ocean

no stars

I inhale
to forget
and forget everything
but where I want to be

Life #6

Doing I CHING

```
_____
___   ___
___   ___
_____
___   ___
_____
```

touching the Divine
listening to Sade
    crooning
            on VH1
smelling the new rain
            through my open screen
        on Washington Street
the spirit moving me
there's enough
in my life
to drive me
to be born
into it
again
and again.

Tea For the Tillerman

The day Cat
Stevens quit rock n' roll
I was rubbing musk

oil on your soft skin
the breeze coming through
the bedroom lace curtains

I was touching you
in the hot summer afternoon
looking for direction

you pointed out
the window   two dogs sniffing noses
then separating

it was a wild world then
carefree   young
that's how I remember it.

Mediterranean Cat

I turned to her   At the same time,
she turned away.   Gulls flew
above the sea.   "You can stay the night,"
she said.   "My husband's away."

Off-season: the incense was patchouli,
candles black, and the cat
looked like a black panther
or a sphinx
from the back.
Her lace pillows overlooked the sea.

I was passing through on a poetry
tour   had known her years before.
Back then I wanted to be Kerouac
traveling with dreams in my knapsack
still do

After we made love
we smoked a joint
like old times
in her Sicily ashtray.

For the first time I understood
how sailors in Egypt
turned wild tigers
to household pets.

Seer Meditating
Near the Ocean, by Candlelight

the black and white cat
on the futon
rests alone, afloat
and safe

purring before
the black candle.

In the wavering light
he sees soul-rodents
of the dead.

There's a smell of fish
and through the window
the moon's beam
pulls up the tide.

He knows all
about the planet,
rats, ghosts, and thunderstorms.

No Longer a Vessel
Like Mozart to God

angelic prophet of wrath
kerouac lookalike
magic powder clings to lips
and cheap gin to the mike
gods give up and hang him from
laces of his Nikes

Amelia Earhart Poem

    in her flyer's cap
   black leather bomber's jacket
khakis and scarf
  she flew through the air
    till the engine stopped in th

                  e

                 c l

              ou

                d

                  s.

Nike Tree

An old white
sneaker hangs
on a red maple tree
near the telephone
    pole
       o
       n

       t
       h
       e

       r
       o
       a
       d

       t
       o

    NYC

Red Cats   Black Cats   Angela Davis

draft cards in duffle bags
ready for the flames
black power fist embroidered on torn
blue denim jacket, peace sign on another
our train thumps
from Syracuse to NYC
for the demonstrations-Black Power, ♀ Power, PEACE
as sunset caresses the smokey haze
over Washington Square.

Expatricat
(after Lavonne Mueller)

I wanted to stay
in NYC
where every morning
the sun
fell through the huge stained
glass window and warmed
my fur.
But no
we had to go to Paris
57 Rue de Fleur
'cause Alice insisted.

I
belonged to the city I left.

Where were the garbage and rodents
when I sniffed piles of chicken bones and skin
and rat's tails and fell asleep in Central Park
tired from the crowds?

France
was a prison to me
Gertrude sat on her fat ass all day
while I
watched Alice bake hash
brownies
sometimes she threw me a crumb
Better than catnip.

In Paris
she let me run my tongue
over all her recipes
then they'd go down to
some trendy cafes
or was it the Quatre Cats Tavern
or was that in Barcelona?
anyway
they'd go there to meet Picasso
and all those other guys.
They'd leave me alone
to sink into slow violin music of the dead
So I'd claw ancient Mayan designs
in their Persian rugs
to get even.

Then they'd return
drunk and obnoxious
Picasso always bragging
What a pompous asshole he was.
Hemingway chasing me
through the house.

When fame came
after all the lust and brownies
it was I
who was snubbed
for a rose

the line originally read—
A cat is a cat is a cat.

Café Expresso, Woodstock, NY

1968 Catskill Saturday Night
bar was packed

crowded for hours
Dylan singing

"Desolation Row"
He was God then

came out, blew 16 bars
on the harmonica

into the audience
into Eternity.

Alchemy

It's always on a grey, Dorothy kind of day
when some wizard comes by banging
on my door
or some rabbit hops by
wanting to take me in a hole somewhere
they make all kinds of promises
like I can be a princess
grow smaller, get richer
and all this other shit
I tell them I'm not one
for Adventure
I'd rather stay here and turn
dizzy blue lines
into gold.

New Orleans

Walking through the French Quarter
filled with jazz on a dog sweltering August day
drinking Hurricanes
smelling chickory coffee and beinets
our stoned minds floating like lemon peels
down the Mississippi

Walking past ghost-filled Southern mansions
and artist-filled Jackson Square
we finally entered the Haunt
of Marie Labeau
new orleans #1 voodoo queen

this was the part of the city
the tourists didn't see
Bodies rotting in below-sea level ground
chicken feet   Dixie cans filled with blood
and skin piled in a rusted cauldron

Drugged, stinking survivors, we crept
away with souvenirs in our bloodstained hands.

Temptation

――――――――
――――――――
――――――――
――――――――
――――   ――――

The (wind) is moving beneath
the creative (heaven)
forming the condition for Temptation
The Book of Changes has warned me.
I suppose I could ignore it
or wear a windbreaker
But it's warned me now.
Here. July 1.

3 a.m.   I'm at Geno's Bar
with you wondering
why I'm here   the day flew
I haven't spent
any time writing
the wind caresses me   then divides.

5 a.m.   the guilt sets in
watching ANTONIO'S LINE together
best foreign film
on my VCR
I held your hand and
saw the blood.

Summer of '96

> "You and I dance real slow-we
> got nowhere to go."—Melissa Etheridge

The sea
twisting loose from
its boundaries. A book
of Sarton's poetry by
your bed, sunlight washing
over the room.   These
days, the simple things
please us. The wine in its
thick goblets,
or poems left unfinished
or the sound of ocean waves
lapping the shore.

You're listening to Melissa, to
the seagulls opening
and closing the white closet
of their wings—the same
closet where
they keep their strength.

This summer you ask
me to teach you some
Rich, Sexton, Plath
I agree
as I wash my desires
into the ocean.
This soulful relationship
is fine for now—
hours of conversations, music, poetry,
and third world movies

Settling for your
energy—your fingers
are torches
lighting my creativity
ecstatic at
any touch you give
me though I know
your future lies
with some professor in Tibet.

Letter to a Younger Woman
  (to stryk)

I always felt
love and rejection enhanced
my poetry—made it possible
maybe that's why I kept falling in love
with the wrong women

my quirky ways, my
Bohemian stance
must have won you
at first

agonizing over lines
in a cold room
in Syracuse, I fantasized
about us together
in a warm tub
with candles & Mozart & wine

Now reading Gertrude's Letters
to Alice
I feel crazy.   I wanted

more from you than you
were willing to give: a reason,
an inspiration, the flame
to make my art possible.

Emily Dickinson in
Creative Writing 401

First off
they would have said
Get rid of those horizontal lines—
at the end of your sentences.
What do they mean?
If you want to get published
you can't use them.

Next
get rid of those huge words
like Destiny, Beauty, Fate
Be more specific for Christ's sake.

And finally
Emily get out of the house
seek adventure
perhaps a grad course
in London instead of staying in
and writing about Death.

The Self-Indulgence of An Outsider
  (to Colin Wilson)

Reading: "The Tarot"

Significator: The Hermit
    1.   The Devil
    2.   Temptation
    3.   Death

       Meditation

To learn to live alone
          with pain

          my black cat dreams that his tail
          has become a serpent

   watch myself self-destruct
   under a bottle of tequila
   to sleep with men and women
   and never come
   to listen to Gershwin blues
   all night in seedy bars
   cruising women
   craving only those I cannot have
   to live an   occult life
   and fuck with demons.

   to never be satisfied.

I burn

   incense and make offerings

   to Eros
   then turn
      to poetry
   as a last resort
        before Suicide.

Jesus

You get out of bed each morning
and pray.

I drink coffee
+ read the Times.

You worry that I'm not enlightened
stuck on some lower level
"But do you have any scriptures
to pray me out of this?" I ask.

You touch my forehead
mumble some words
then put on your blue Levi's
and green holy workshirt from
The Salvation Army.

As you drink your
young red wine
and eat your fresh
baked bread
you shake your head
and realize that
I can't even find my way
from the breadbox to the toaster.

Reading a Chinese
Calendar While Waiting
In Line at Hunan's Restaurant

1996
This is the year of the RAT
Newt, Dole, Gramm, Helms, Rush

Syracuse, Without Snow or Spirituality
    (to Eliot Schain)

Whenever Robert Bly comes
to read poetry in Syracuse
it snows, so I go home disappointed
order a pizza, drink beer
or read Tarot cards with the psychic
next door who only predicts
more snow. She is a nice woman
an earth woman who gardens cooks sews
But I want something more,
I want a young woman
who howls at the moon
who's never heard of SILENCE IN THE SNOWY FIELDS,
mantras, pop art, Crumb or The Velvet Underground.

Affair on X-mas Eve

Drinking Ciro wine
on the floor mattress

Drunk with the scent
of you, x-mas
balsam, vanilla candles and
long kisses

your earring falls on the floor.

There's mischief here
as you lie beside me

let's put our treasures aside;
shoot for a single soul. Simplicity

is key my dear.
We are together all day

until the sun goes away
and
will you come
back at midnight?

Black Cats in the Night

I see two black scroungy cats
fighting over a Colonel
Sanders chicken bone
I threw in the gutter
last night on my way home
from your apartment
they reminded me of Top Cat
and the other
cartoon cats
I used to watch as a child
mangy cats hanging out by
garbage cans
fighting for their territory
like you and me earlier
stray cats thrown together
before a fire
submerged in the glow
eyes young and wild
yet holding back
always afraid
to give up.

Kafka

Last night I dreamt
I became a giant beetle.
It's been a year since I've worked
It's been a long Sunday
spent in bed.
The last time I tried
to get out of bed I fell
and broke my leg.
You and the charwoman left
and I spent my days
watching a door
opening and closing
on death.

Sleeping in the House
Of Gertrude and Alice

Today, a little tired, this day
I am up early and asking
How much of the Amazon do I own?
And who locked the bedroom door?

6 A.M.
Two hours before sesame bagels and coffee
and in the house of two women.
I lie still   nothing happens.
I figure my choices
and hold to my course.

> In the house of two women
> the bubble bath, the powders, the brushes
> are all political things.

At 8:15 I vomit,
meditate
and yet hold still

in the house of two women

where time drags
in lavender air.

Passion

BLONDE ON BLONDE
on the stereo
a day of desire
thighs opening and closing
stopping only to eat
strawberries
flakes of snow slowly
drifting outside the window
I will love you all day
and night   won't stop it
will never stop it
until you scream enough
radiators banging
chipmunks racing
through the walls
the neighbor's stereo blasting—
music to love you by
all part of the dance
let's tango in the shadows
our sweaty bodies intertwined
let's die in the height of passion
it's getting harder and harder
to leave you. It's getting harder
and harder to go back
home.

Threesome

Out of the middle
It is cold out here. Ber-
muda Triangle

Leaping II

reading Robert Bly
leaping to a sorrowful
riff from Coltrane's sax

Frog
   (to lew welch)

Think what would happen if Munch ever experienced
         Prozac

Or knew 6 campsites in this forest where nobody ever goes
         firewood everywhere   emus for sale   shale   slate

I give you my town of daemons and woodstove-smoke
         cabins where I could love you 6 slow ways.
You who dream of suicide and claim to want eternity.

I sit on a tree stump reading
         Munch's autobiography
throw stones into the water
         like you he wouldn't let anyone near him.

I learned a new thing today—
         most geniuses are either neurotic or psychotic
         or suicidal

I put on the frog ring you gave me
         from Provincetown—a place where the moon
is even wilder than you think   there is
         just one frog   and a light we could lie by
where eternity is the ocean meeting the sky

Shattered
More than in that Norwegian's sad eye
         you tell me that love doesn't exist
yet in the next breath you ask me
         if I love you
so many contradictions

I'd like to be the poet of the 21st century—
         the poet whose verse
gets stones moving across the sea
         I'd like to go a new route and see
everything in a new light—
         an ocean's light

I put on my clean shorts
         and think of Munch—
they thought he was crazy
         because he saw it all
so clearly
         just like you.

Park Bench

On a park bench on a Syracuse night
with a dog and cup of vanilla
coffee
we watched lights off the parkway.
After a poetry reading
with you striding beside me
we wandered
beneath streetlights
We passed dark houses
three barking dogs
two squirrels
we discussed Rimbaud
in the moonlight
haunted by the ghost of the drunken poet
I carry my inspiration
from old abbeys
to dark bars
afternoon drifts into evening
I hid your souvenirs and prophecies
in tattered poetry books
I still think of you as I sit alone
on a dark green bench in Onondaga Parkway.

I Awoke at 3AM
         (to Senghor)

I awoke at 3AM beneath the April rain,
and in the night I saw a winged horse,
panthers, a snake eating clear through
    my soul.
I lay there for an hour, musing over visions.
Your visions, singing your last words
Your black coffin and the closed door of goodbye.

I awoke in the air of frankincense, exquisite scents,
your soft lips, your face smooth as a child's
like Rimbaud's angelic stare. Your voice
ringing like church bells or sun at the window
this new morning.
And ascending everywhere from light and darkness,
were your smells of wild
musk
Diluted by tears.

A Night With a Rimbaudian Poet
    after Arlene Biala

You pick up the glass of absinthe
    and toast to yourself

then you recite Rimbaud's

    Seasons in Hell to me
    in bed

    I pick up the half-full bottle
    and pour

        We talk of Verlaine +
        Rimbaud's turbulent relationship
        shooting and stabbing each other
        arguing all the time
        yet creating the best poetry
        when they were together.

We finish off the bottle

        I reach for you.
        "I want to go beyond
        the sexual level," you say.
        "Your soul will only suffer from
        your obsession with sex."

I agree but can't stop.

"We are like Rimbaud and Verlaine
reincarnated. We are Companions in Hell,"
I say as I put the movie
"Total Eclipse" into the VCR.

        You pick up the empty bottle
        and toss it against the wall,
            take a piece of glass
               and rip open my wrist.

            Another poem.

I See the I CHING

I see the I CHING tattoo on your leg
pointing The Way

I feel the sweat inside my Nike Air sneakers
pouring out into a sea of darkness.

Both Hands

Both hands clenched
Disjointed nervous smile trapped between them

Like one of those women
in a Picasso painting.

Turtle Meditates

Turtle meditates
on rock at Erie Canal
then plunges in mud.

Perfect

Sitting before the woodstove
in a Pendleton jacket
I thumb through
pages of my book of days

I feel like Aleister Crowley's
black cat
mysterious
full of magic
clawing up my 9-Lives.

I smoke joint after joint
write a great poem
then fall asleep on my futon.

This is the life I've chosen
not feeling guilty
about anything
knowing
even the 8th century Zen
Buddhist monk Huai-su liked
to work when drunk
on rice wine.

Amelia or
April 10, 1997

In your bomber jacket
wing pin on the collar
Brando t-shirt and jeans
you washed down valium
with Old Crow and beer
+ watched Hale-Bopp
stream across the sky.

I made a Monte Cristo sandwich
drank 1977 Beaujolais
and read the second half of WAR AND PEACE
Found myself in the April moonlight
charting the astrological distances
between us.

Poet in a Dunescape

It began with sand,
then came the clamshell path,
the lobster-traps, with seaweed around them,
the leaky-drinking trough under the acadia tree
where giraffes used to stand
amidst rippled grasses

Then came night
that was like dripping water.
At times, for days
a spirit flew,
half bird, half horse
just above the straw roof
from where a coyote howled.

It was there
she forgot about death
on the tattered rice paper
the flickering candlelight in the window.

Cloisters

Like a monk she strolls through the cloisters
she walks past medieval tapestries of unicorns and hunters
feeling the abbey's cold draft through her bones

Her poems are absorbed in fables of Death
as she walks past jousting tournament scenes above her head
like a monk she strolls through the cloisters

the sadness...oh god only knows
as she dreams Hildegard's visions
feeling the abbey's cold draft through her bones

In the morning she'll listen to Gregorian Chants
drink Emperor's Choice herbal tea
Like a monk she strolls through the cloisters

In her mind a forest seems to grow
she leaves shadows against the cobbled stones.
Feeling the abbey's cold draft through her bones

And she sleeps through sculptured tunnels
becomes elated temporarily and wards off her obsession with
Death
Like a monk she wanders through the cloisters
feeling the abbey's cold through her bones.

Printed in the United States
By Bookmasters